A Home
for Me

Apartment

Lola M. Schaefer

Heinemann Library
Chicago, Illinois

©2003 Reed Educational & Professional Publishing
Published by Heinemann Library,
an imprint of Reed Educational & Professional Publishing
Chicago, IL

Customer Service 888-454-2279
Visit our website at www.heinemannlibrary.com

Designed by Sue Emerson, Heinemann Library
Printed and bound in the United States by Lake Book Manufacturing, Inc.

07 06 05 04 03
10 9 8 7 6 5 4 3 2 1

Library of Congress Cataloging-in-Publication Data
Lola M. Schaefer
    Apartment / Lola M. Schaefer.
        p. cm. — (A Home for Me)
Includes index.
Summary: Contents: What is an apartment?—What do apartment buildings look like?—How big are apartments?—How many rooms are in an apartment?—Where do people talk and play in an apartment?—Where do people cook in an apartment?—Where do people sleep in an apartment?—Where do people bathe in an apartment?—Where do people who live in an apartment clean their clothes?—Apartment map quiz—Apartment picture glossary.
    ISBN: 1-4034-0258-2 (HC), 1-4034-0481-X (Pbk.)
    1. Apartments—Juvenile literature. Apartment houses—Juvenile literature. [1. Apartments. 2. Apartment houses.]
    I. Title. II. Series: Schaefer, Lola M., 1950–. Home for me.
    GT172.S325 2002
    643'.2—dc21

2001008141

Acknowledgments
The author and publishers are grateful to the following for permission to reproduce copyright material:
p. 4 Rudi Von Briel/Index Stock Imagery; pp. 5, 12, 14, 17, 18, 19, 20 Robert Lifson/ Heinemann Library; pp. 6, 15 Jill Birschbach/Heinemann Library; p. 7 David June; p. 8 Michael Boys/Corbis; p. 9 Karen Bussolini; p. 13 Spike Powell, Elizabeth Whiting & Associates/Corbis; p. 16 Charles Cook; p. 21 Greg Williams/Heinemann Library; p. 23 (row 1, L-R) David June, Greg Williams/Heinemann Library, Robert Lifson/Heinemann Library; p. 23 (row 2, L-R) Jill Birschbach/ Heinemann Library, Robert Lifson/Heinemann Library; p. 23 (row 3, L-R) Robert Folz/Visuals Unlimited, Jill Birschbach/ Heinemann Library; back cover David June

Cover photograph Perry Mastrovito/Corbis
Photo research by Amor Montes de Oca
Special thanks to our models, the Ryan family, and to Chuck and Jennifer Gillis for the use of their apartment.

Special thanks to our advisory panel for their help in the preparation of this book:

Eileen Day, Preschool teacher
Chicago, IL

Ellen Dolmetsch,
Library Media Specialist
Wilmington, DE

Kathleen Gilbert,
Second Grade Teacher
Round Rock, TX

Sandra Gilbert,
Library Media Specialist
Houston, TX

Angela Leeper,
Educational Consultant
North Carolina Department
of Public Instruction
Raleigh, NC

Pam McDonald,
Reading Support Specialist
Winter Springs, FL

Melinda Murphy,
Library Media Specialist
Houston, TX

Some words are shown in bold, **like this.**
You can find them in the picture glossary on page 23.

Contents

What Is an Apartment?

An apartment is a group of rooms that people live in.

The rooms are close together.

There are many apartments in an **apartment building.**

Many families live in one building.

What Do Apartment Buildings Look Like?

Some **apartment buildings** are short and wide.

There may be **patios** or **balconies** outside.

Some apartment buildings are tall and narrow.

They have many different floors.

How Big Are Apartments?

Apartments can be big or small.

In some apartments, everything fits in one room.

But some apartments even have
an upstairs and a downstairs!

How Many Rooms Are in an Apartment?

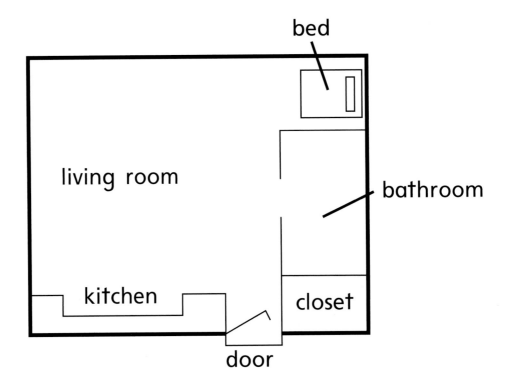

bed

living room

bathroom

kitchen

closet

door

Some apartments may have only one or two rooms.

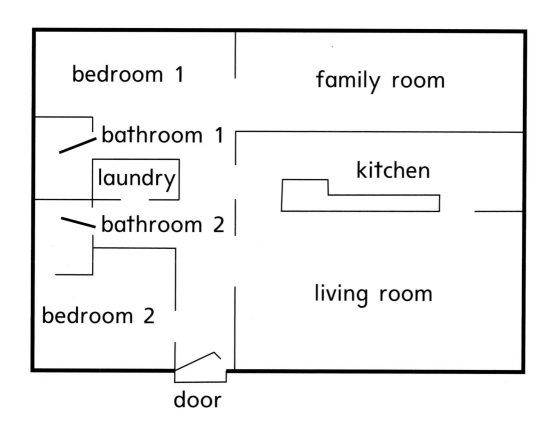

bedroom 1

bathroom 1

laundry

bathroom 2

bedroom 2

family room

kitchen

living room

door

Large apartments may have six
rooms or more.

Where Do People Talk and Play?

People talk and play in the living room.

They may watch television there, too.

Living rooms have a sofa, chairs, tables, and lamps.

Where Do People Cook and Eat?

People cook in the kitchen.

Sometimes there is a place to eat in the kitchen.

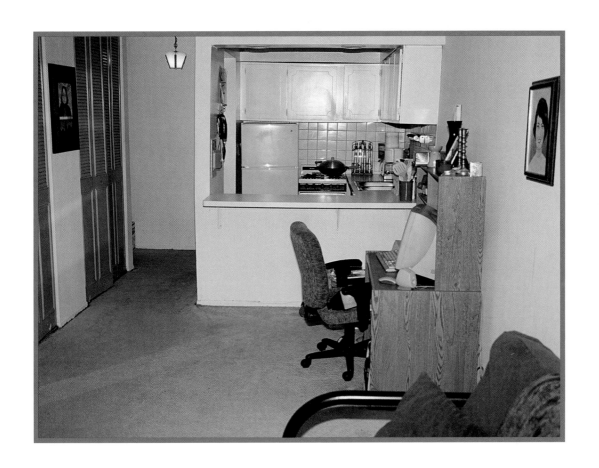

Some apartments are just one room.

There is a small kitchen in the room.

Where Do People Sleep?

Most people sleep in bedrooms.

Bedrooms have beds, **dressers,** and closets.

Some small apartments only have
one bedroom.

Then, people may sleep on a
sofa bed.

Where Do People Take Baths?

Apartments have a bathroom.

People take showers or baths there.

Every bathroom has a sink and
a toilet, too.

Sometimes there is more than one
bathroom in an apartment.

Where Do People Wash Their Clothes?

Some people wash their clothes in their apartment.

They have a **washing machine** and a **dryer** in a closet.

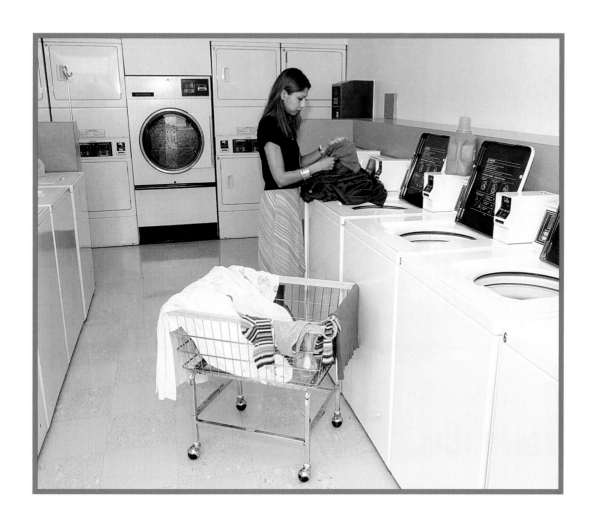

Some **apartment buildings** have a laundry room.

People wash and dry their clothes there.

Map Quiz

How many bedrooms are in this apartment?

What is the small room next to each bedroom?

Look for the answers on page 24.

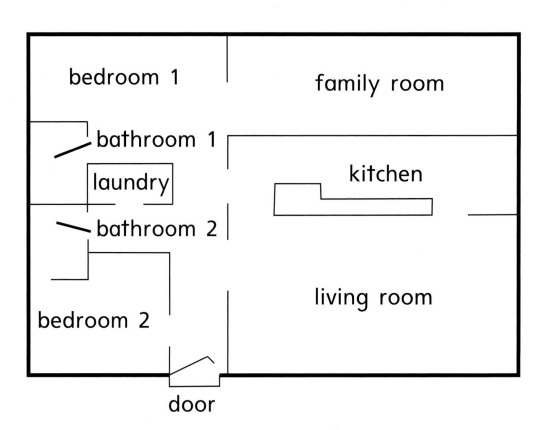

bedroom 1

family room

bathroom 1

laundry

kitchen

bathroom 2

bedroom 2

living room

door

Picture Glossary

apartment building
pages 5, 6, 7, 21

dryer
page 20

sofa bed
page 17

balcony
page 6

patio
page 6

washing machine
page 20

dresser
page 16

Note to Parents and Teachers

Reading for information is an important part of a child's literacy development. Learning begins with a question about something. Help children think of themselves as investigators and researchers by encouraging their questions about the world around them. Each chapter in this book begins with a question. Read the question together. Look at the pictures. Talk about what you think the answer might be. Then read the text to find out if your predictions were correct. Think of other questions you could ask about the topic, and discuss where you might find the answers. Use the two simple maps on pages 10 and 11 to introduce children to basic map-reading skills. After discussing the maps, help children draw their own map of a familiar place, such as their room. Assist children in using the picture glossary and the index to practice new vocabulary and research skills.

Index

Answers to quiz on page 22

There are two bedrooms in this apartment.

There is a bathroom next to each bedroom.